GO AHEAD-MAKE ME LAUGH

.

Meridith Berk & Toni Vavrus
Illustrated by Jeff Sinclair

FLUFFY

 Sterling Publishing Co., Inc.   New York

Library of Congress Cataloging-in-Publication Data

Berk, Meridith.
  Go ahead—make me laugh / Meridith Berk & Toni Vavrus ; illus-
trated by Jeff Sinclair.
     p.   cm.
  Includes index.
  Summary: A collection of jokes and riddles, including knock-knocks,
put-downs, tricky jokes, tongue twisters, and "ridiculous" riddles.
  ISBN 0-8069-8442-2
  1. Wit and humor, Juvenile. [1. Jokes. 2. Riddles.] I. Vavrus,
Toni. II. Sinclair, Jeff, ill. III. Title.
PN6163.B38   1992
818'.5402—dc20
                                                      91-48261
                                                        CIP
                                                         AC

A Special Edition of Willowisp Press, a division of PAGES, Inc.

      6   8   10 9   7   5   3   1

       k edition published in 1993 by
       ing Company, Inc.
       uth, New York, N.Y. 10016
       & Toni Vavrus
       nclair
       rling Publishing

      anadian Manda Group, P.O. Box 920, Station U
Toronto, Ontario, Canada M8Z 5P9
Distributed in Great Britain and Europe by Cassell PLC
Villiers House, 41/47 Strand, London WC2N 5JE, England
Distributed in Australia by Capricorn Link Ltd.
P.O. Box 665, Lane Cove, NSW 2066
Manufactured in the United States of America
All rights reserved

Sterling ISBN 0-8069-8442-2 Trade
             0-8069-8443-0 Paper

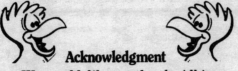

Acknowledgment

We would like to thank Albie Berk for his help in writing this book. Albie, you "have the gift."

Contents

1
All-Star Animal Riddles

What's worse than finding a worm in your apple?
Finding a frog in your throat.

What would you get if you crossed a frog and a chameleon?
Leaping lizards.

Why is it so hard to make frogs cry?
They're always hoppy.

Why did the rabbit stop hopping?
It was out of bounds.

Why are rabbits so good at arithmetic?
They've had a lot of practice multiplying.

What do you call a rabbit who runs away from home?
Hare today, gone tomorrow.

What kind of bird always sounds cheerful?
A hummingbird.

Where do owls stay when they go on trips?
Hootels.

Did you hear about the owl who married a goat?
They had a hootenanny.

What do you call two keets?
Parakeets.

Why was the chicken booed off the stage?
She laid an egg.

How can you tell a spring chicken?
By the bounce in its step.

What is the most religious bird?
A bird of pray.

Why did the pigeon wear corrective shoes?
He was human-toed.

What do you call a puppy who eats fruit?
A melon collie baby.

What kind of dog takes care of children?
A baby setter.

Why does a dog turn around three times before he lies down?
Because he can't do it after he lies down.

How did Mary keep track of all her lambs?
By hook or by crook.

Why don't you see pigs wandering around the town?
Because they sty at home.

Why can't a foal talk?
Because it's a little hoarse.

Why was the rodeo horse so rich?
He had a lot of bucks in him.

When is the toughest time to play horseshoes?
When the shoes are still on the horses.

What do you get when you cross a mustang with an elephant?
A sports car with plenty of trunk space.

When is a bear most likely to enter your house?
When the door is open.

Why were the lions in the circus no good at tricks?
Because they did so much lion around.

What do you call a well-dressed turtle?
A dapper snapper.

How does a crab become successful?
He claws his way to the top.

What ocean animals go to Hollywood?
Star fish.

What kinds of fish do birds sit on?
Perch.

Why did the fisherman produce such a good movie?
He had a great cast.

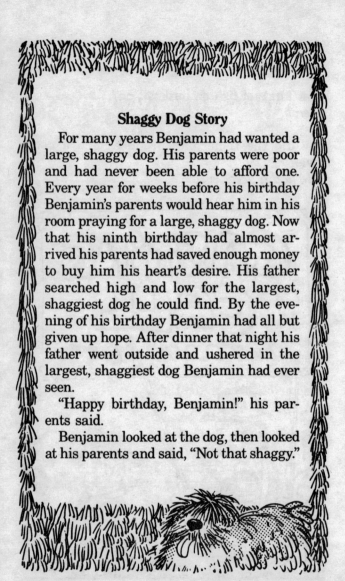

Shaggy Dog Story

For many years Benjamin had wanted a large, shaggy dog. His parents were poor and had never been able to afford one. Every year for weeks before his birthday Benjamin's parents would hear him in his room praying for a large, shaggy dog. Now that his ninth birthday had almost arrived his parents had saved enough money to buy him his heart's desire. His father searched high and low for the largest, shaggiest dog he could find. By the evening of his birthday Benjamin had all but given up hope. After dinner that night his father went outside and ushered in the largest, shaggiest dog Benjamin had ever seen.

"Happy birthday, Benjamin!" his parents said.

Benjamin looked at the dog, then looked at his parents and said, "Not that shaggy."

2
Who's That Knocking at My Door?

Knock knock.
  Who's there?
Despair.
  Despair who?
Despair of shoes is too tight.

          Knock knock.
              Who's there?
          Panther.
              Panther who?
          My panther ripped down the thide.

Knock knock.
  Who's there?
Ivanhoe.
  Ivanhoe who?
Ivanhoe, want me to do your yard work?

Knock knock.
   Who's there?
Canoe.
   Canoe who?
Canoe open the door for me?

Knock knock.
   Who's there?
Norma Lee.
   Norma Lee who?
Norma Lee I don't ring other people's doorbells.

Knock knock.
   Who's there?
Shirley.
   Shirley who?
Shirley you know my last name by this time.

Knock knock.
  Who's there?
Mango.
  Mango who?
Mango down hall. Me follow.

Knock knock.
  Who's there?
Ben.
  Ben who?
Ben looking all over for you.

Knock knock.
  Who's there?
Doughnut.
  Doughnut who?
Doughnut bother me
with silly questions!

Knock knock.
  Who's there?
Sow.
  Sow who?
Sow ya doing?

Knock knock.
  Who's there?
Barry.
  Barry who?
Barry good of you to answer the door.

Knock knock.
Who's there?
Randolph.
Randolph who?
Randolph (ran off) without my key.

Knock knock.
Who's there?
Red Denny.
Red who?
Red Denny good books lately?

Knock knock.
Who's there?
Xavier.
Xavier who?
Xavier (save your) money.

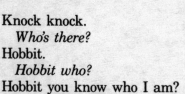

Knock knock.
Who's there?
Hobbit.
Hobbit who?
Hobbit you know who I am?

Knock knock.
Who's there?
Bea Levitt.
Bea Levitt who?
Bea Levitt it or not, I want to come in.

Knock knock.
  Who's there?
Elias.
  Elias who?
Elias (he lies) like a trooper.

Knock knock.
  Who's there?
Naomi.
  Naomi who?
Naomi some money, but they won't pay.

Knock knock.
  Who's there?
Noah.
  Noah who?
Noah-counting for taste.

Knock knock.
  Who's there?
Justin.
  Justin who?
Justin time for dinner.

Knock knock.
  Who's there?
Distressing.
  Distressing who?
Distressing has too much vinegar.

Knock knock.
  Who's there?
Gnu.
  Gnu who?
Gnu kid on the block.

Knock knock.
  Who's there?
Madeline.
  Madeline who?
Madeline (madder than) a wet hen.

Knock knock.
  Who's there?
Raoul.
  Raoul who?
Raoul out the barrel!

Knock knock.
  Who's there?
Barry.
  Barry who?
"Barry (Bury) me not on the lone prairie . . ."

Knock knock.
  Who's there?
Alaska.
  Alaska who?
Alaska another one later.

18

Knock knock.
Who's there?
Carla.
Carla who?
Carla locksmith. My key won't work.

Knock knock.
Who's there?
Whirly.
Whirly who?
"Whirly to bed, whirly to rise . . ."

Knock knock.
Who's there?
Meyer.
Meyer who?
Meyer nosey!

Knock knock.
Who's there?
July.
July who?
July like a trooper.

Knock knock.
Who's there?
Toupee.
Toupee who?
"Toupee or not toupee—that is the question."

Knock knock.
  Who's there?
Saddle.
  Saddle who?
Saddle be the day!

Knock knock.
  Who's there?
Sumatra.
  Sumatra who?
Sumatra day I'll call you.

Knock knock.
  Who's there?
Iona.
  Iona who?
Iona house on this block.

Knock knock.
  Who's there?
Hugh.
  Hugh who?
"Hugh better watch out, you better not cry . . ."

Knock knock.
  Who's there?
Farmer.
  Farmer who?
Farmer (far more) people knock on doors
these days.

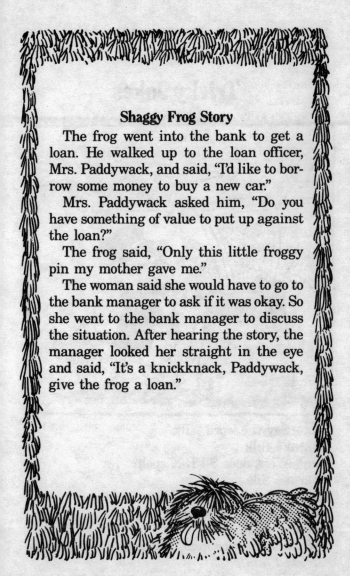

Shaggy Frog Story

The frog went into the bank to get a loan. He walked up to the loan officer, Mrs. Paddywack, and said, "I'd like to borrow some money to buy a new car."

Mrs. Paddywack asked him, "Do you have something of value to put up against the loan?"

The frog said, "Only this little froggy pin my mother gave me."

The woman said she would have to go to the bank manager to ask if it was okay. So she went to the bank manager to discuss the situation. After hearing the story, the manager looked her straight in the eye and said, "It's a knickknack, Paddywack, give the frog a loan."

3
Tricky Jokes

YOU: Say the word "silk."

FRIEND: Silk.

YOU: What does S-I-L-K spell?

FRIEND: Silk.

Do this several times. Then:

YOU: What do cows drink?

FRIEND: Milk.

(Since cows give milk, but don't drink it, you've tricked him!)

Here are some more tricky jokes:

YOU: Say the word "folk."
FRIEND: Folk.
YOU: What does F-O-L-K spell?
FRIEND: Folk.
Do this several times. Then:
YOU: What is the white part of an egg called?
FRIEND: Yolk.
(Since the yellow part of the egg is called the yolk, you've tricked her!)

YOU: Ask me if I'm a lion.
FRIEND: Are you a lion?
YOU: Yes. Ask me if I'm a mouse.
FRIEND: Are you a mouse?
YOU: No, didn't I just tell you I was a lion?

SQUEAK TO ME!!

YOU: I bet I can make you say purple.
FRIEND: No, you can't.
YOU: What color is the U.S. flag?
FRIEND: Red, white and blue.
YOU: You see? I told you I could make you say red!
FRIEND: No—I could say red. I wasn't supposed to say purple!
YOU: You see? I made you say it!

23

YOU: How do you spell "go"?
FRIEND: G-O.
YOU: What does G-O spell?
FRIEND: Go.

Do this several times. Then:

YOU: Would you like some candy?
FRIEND *(usually answers):* No.

YOU: How do you spell "rope"?
FRIEND: R-O-P-E.
YOU: What does R-O-P-E spell?
FRIEND: Rope.

Do this several times. Then:

YOU: What do you call a smart person?
FRIEND *(will usually answer):* Dope.

YOU: What does M-A-C-D-O-N-A-L-D spell?
FRIEND: MacDonald.
YOU: What does M-A-C-G-R-E-G-O-R spell?
FRIEND: MacGregor.
YOU: What does M-A-C-H-I-N-E-R-Y spell?
FRIEND *(will probably not realize word is "machinery"):* MacHinery.

YOU: What does O-T-O-O-L-E spell?
FRIEND: O'Toole.
YOU: What does O-M-A-L-L-E-Y spell?
FRIEND: O'Malley.
YOU: What does O-L-I-V-E-R spell?
FRIEND *(will probably not realize name is "Oliver"):* O'Liver.

YOU: What does T-O-U-G-H spell?
FRIEND: Tough.
YOU: What does R-O-U-G-H spell?
FRIEND: Rough.
YOU: What does D-O-U-G-H spell?
FRIEND (*will probably say*): Duff.

YOU: There were two farms next to each other. One was in Canada and one was in the United States. A rooster ran from the farm in Canada to the farm in the United States and laid an egg. To which country did the egg belong?
FRIEND (*wrong no matter which country he says.*) (*The answer is: No one. Roosters don't lay eggs.*)

YOU: If a chicken laid an egg on the border between France and Russia, to which country would the egg belong?

FRIEND *(wrong no matter which country she says).* *(The answer is: Neither. These countries don't border on each other.)*

YOU: Which is correct: the white of an egg *is* yellow. The white of an egg *are* yellow.

FRIEND *(will probably say):* The white of an egg is yellow.

(The answer is: Neither. The white of an egg is white.)

YOU: Would you like to learn some magical words of the mysterious East?

FRIEND: Okay.

YOU: Repeat after me: O wah ta goo Siam.

FRIEND: Oh, what a goose I am.

YOU: Just keep repeating that . . .

O WAH TA GOO SIAM
O WAH TA GOO SIAM
O WAH TA GOO SIAM
O WAH TA GOO SIAM
O WAH TA GOO SIAM
O WAH TA GOO SIAM
O WAH TA GOO SIAM

YOU: Pete and Repeat went for a boat ride. Pete fell in. Who was left?

FRIEND: Repeat.

YOU: Pete and Repeat went for a boat ride. Pete fell in. Who was left?

(And you keep on repeating it, too.)

YOU: Say "Pen."

FRIEND: Pen.

YOU: Say "Men."

FRIEND: Men.

YOU: Say "Ben."

FRIEND: Ben.

YOU: What are aluminum cans made of?

FRIEND *(will probably say):* Tin.

YOU: Say "Host."

FRIEND: Host.

YOU: Say "Most."

FRIEND: Most.

YOU: Say "Post."

FRIEND: Post.

YOU: What do you put in a toaster?

FRIEND *(will probably say):* Toast.

YOU: What does L-O-V-E spell?

FRIEND: Love.

YOU: What does G-L-O-V-E spell?

FRIEND: Glove.

YOU: What does D-O-V-E spell?

FRIEND: Dove.

YOU: What does M-O-V-E spell?

FRIEND *(will probably say):* Muv.

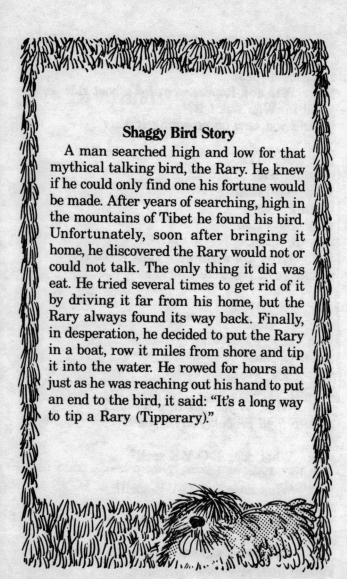

Shaggy Bird Story

A man searched high and low for that mythical talking bird, the Rary. He knew if he could only find one his fortune would be made. After years of searching, high in the mountains of Tibet he found his bird. Unfortunately, soon after bringing it home, he discovered the Rary would not or could not talk. The only thing it did was eat. He tried several times to get rid of it by driving it far from his home, but the Rary always found its way back. Finally, in desperation, he decided to put the Rary in a boat, row it miles from shore and tip it into the water. He rowed for hours and just as he was reaching out his hand to put an end to the bird, it said: "It's a long way to tip a Rary (Tipperary)."

4
Putdowns, Insults & Comebacks

You have a face only Frankenstein's mother could love.

The day you were born your parents cried like babies.

You couldn't win if they tied you to the finish line.

If you were the last person alive, the world would still be overpopulated.

Little old ladies won't let you help them across the street.

Losing your head would be an improvement on your looks.

Even my dog wouldn't bite you, and he'll eat anything.

In a race with six runners you'd come in seventh.

If you were really smart you'd take the hangers out of your clothes before putting them on.

Calling you a dogface would be an insult to dogs.

When brains were passed out there were none small enough to fit in your head.

You'd look better if you combed your hair over your face.

VERY VERY FEEBLE

He's So Weak . . .

Babies steal candy from him.

He couldn't wind up a conversation.

He can't reach a conclusion.

He can't hold his breath.

He can't rise to an occasion.

The only dumbbell he can lift is himself.

Your idea of an exciting time is to wait for the minute hand on a clock to move.

You're lower than the lint in an earthworm's belly button.

Talking to you is as exciting as lapsing into a coma.

Where's your owner? I thought this city had a leash law.

May I add your head to my rock garden?

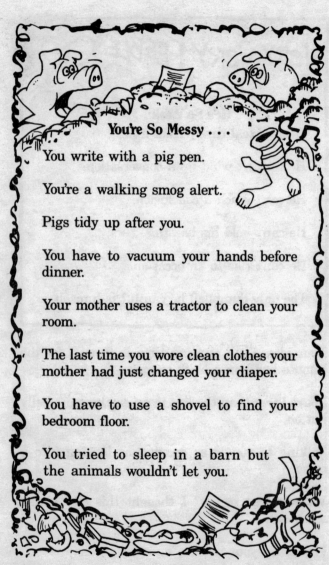

You're So Messy . . .

You write with a pig pen.

You're a walking smog alert.

Pigs tidy up after you.

You have to vacuum your hands before dinner.

Your mother uses a tractor to clean your room.

The last time you wore clean clothes your mother had just changed your diaper.

You have to use a shovel to find your bedroom floor.

You tried to sleep in a barn but the animals wouldn't let you.

He's So Mean . . .

His goldfish ran away from home.

Darth Vader took lessons from him.

Willows weep when he walks by.

He beats his lollipop before he licks it.

He lit a fire in the fireplace on Christmas Eve.

Santa Claus removed him from his address book.

Bananas split when they see him coming.

His parents ran away from home.

When he was born he slapped the doctor.

His family had to tie him up when the mailman came.

Sharks give him professional courtesy.

He's So Lazy . . .

Someone else has to digest his food.

He won't focus his eyes.

His dog has to walk himself.

His hat leaves a tan line at his chin.

He has to prop his eyelids open.

He won't eat anything he has to chew.

He won't snore because it takes too much effort.

He won't even use a remote control.

He refuses to turn his head when he watches a tennis match.

He won't even lift his finger.

He's So Lazy . . .

He hires somebody to breathe for him.

He never gets out of bed—he'd just have to get in it again.

His mother has to prop him up to eat.

He has his brother strike out for him.

He strikes out so he won't have to walk to first base.

His mother has to chew his food for him.

He'll take anything lying down.

He bought elevator shoes so he wouldn't have to walk up the stairs.

He drives his dog for a walk.

He thinks reading is a spectator sport.

He's Such An Airhead . . .

He thought the D on his report card was for Daring.

He thought Arkansas was a carpenter's tool.

He didn't want to take a shower because it wasn't his.

He tried to get a subscription to fly paper.

He thought a bridle path was a wedding aisle.

He oiled his mouse to keep it from squeaking.

He was afraid of flunking his blood test.

Don't give me a piece of your mind—you can't afford it.

The last time you got a date it was at a fruit stand.

Termites must have damaged your brain.

When you were born they broke the mould, purposely.

You can't change your mind. How can you change something you don't have?

You're like an unsharpened pencil, you never come to the point.

You're so low you look up to worms.

On Halloween are you going to dress up like a person?

Shaggy Mole Story

In a kingdom far away there lived a palace gardener named Lucas. Lucas kept the gardens beautifully. The flowers bloomed, weeds were pulled, and vegetables and fruit were abundant. Only one problem detracted from the beauty of the gardens. For years a mole had made them his home. He'd been around so long that the palace staff named him Joel.

One day the king tripped over one too many molehills. He called Lucas into his chambers and ordered him to get rid of the mole. Lucas started off sure it would be an easy task. But over the years Joel had grown to gigantic proportions and nothing Lucas did could get rid of him. After months had passed the king called Lucas before him, demanding an explanation. Lucas looked at him sadly and said, "Oh, King, Joel is a scary old mole."

5
Good News/Bad News

The good news is your mom bought ice cream for dessert.

The bad news is it melted on the way home.

The good news is your class is going on a field trip to a candy factory.

The bad news is you just came down with the measles.

The good news is today is your birthday.

The bad news is no one remembered.

The good news is school is closed because of the snowstorm.

The bad news is you have to shovel the walk.

The good news is you found a dozen Easter eggs.
The bad news is they weren't hard-boiled.

The good news is you gave flowers to the prettiest girl in school.
The bad news is they gave her hay fever.

The good news is your best friend gets to sleep over.
The bad news is he snores.

The good news is you finished your science project.
The bad news is it's a week late.

The good news is ten people from your class get to meet the president.
The bad news is you're not one of them.

The good news is my teacher wants me to join the marching band.
The bad news is I play the cello.

The good news is you got out of class for a fire drill.
The bad news is it was during lunch hour.

The good news is there is a new boy in school.
The bad news is he's my brother.

The good news is I got a new clock radio.
The bad news is it wakes me up at six a.m.

The good news is I got a dozen presents for my birthday.
The bad news is twelve of them were sweaters.

The good news is I'm studying a foreign language.
The bad news is it's Greek to me.

The good news is I got a part in the school play.
The bad news is I'm a tree.

The good news is we just got a new boat.
The bad news is we live in the desert.

The good news is my father just doubled my allowance.
The bad news is two times zero is zero.

The good news is my father did my history for me.
The bad news is he thinks Abraham Lincoln is still president.

The good news is I'm sure to graduate first grade this year.
The bad news is I'm eleven.

The good news is we just got a fireplace put in the living room.
The bad news is we live in Hawaii.

The good news is school just closed for the summer.
The bad news is the teacher gave me three months of homework.

The good news is I wrote an "A" paper.
The bad news is the teacher lost it.

The good news is I get to sing a solo.
The bad news is I have laryngitis.

The good news is you don't have to go to the doctor.
The bad news is he's coming to you.

The good news is your parents will pay for a movie.
The bad news is you have to take your little sister.

The good news is you have the best grades in your class.
The bad news is you're getting a "D."

The good news is you've inherited a million dollars.
The bad news is you can't get it until you're forty-five.

The good news is the prettiest girl in class wants to go steady with you.
The bad news is she's moving three thousand miles away.

The good news is your parents said you could stay up until midnight.

The bad news is when you're twenty-one.

The good news is you won the race.

The bad news is no one else was in it.

The good news is your father's going to teach you to drive.

The bad news is you're starting with a tricycle.

Fiction Bestseller List

1. *Green Mansions*
   by Manny Rumes

2. *The Longest Day*
   by E. Ternity

3. *The Lost Treasure*
   by Miss Place Tate

4. *The Old Bed*
   by Rusty Springs

5. *The Chinese Spy*
   by I. C. Yu

6. *Sandcastles*
   by C. Shaw

7. *River in the Fog*
   by Miss D. Waters

8. *Dirt, Dust & Grime*
   by Phil Thee

9. *Where's That Girl?*
   by Mister Again

10. *How Do I Get In?*
    by O. Ben Sesame

6
Ridiculous Riddles

What battery gets the best grades in school?
The triple A.

What do you call two bikes that look exactly alike?
Identical Schwinns.

Have you heard about the great new Chinese take-out place?
The Wok Inn.

What do you call an outfielder on a baseball team?
A flycatcher.

Why do criminals make the best bartenders?
They're used to being behind bars.

Why did all the doctors leave the hospital?
The surgeon had all the business sewn up.

What is the difference between the North Pole and the South Pole?
They're a world apart.

Why was the girl afraid to go to finishing school?
She thought it would be the end of her.

Why is tennis such a noisy sport?
You can't play it without raising a racket.

How do you make a cigarette lighter?
Remove the tobacco.

Why are tomatoes the slowest fruit?
They're always trying to ketchup.

Why is hamburger like dirt?
They're both ground.

Why does a chimney sweep like cleaning chimneys?
It soots (suits) him.

Why was the boxer so thirsty after the party?
Everyone beat him to the punch.

Why do people in Dallas need more money than other people?
They pay more Texas.

Why is it wrong to break windows?
Because it causes them pane (pain).

What do you call a house for small people in Alaska?
A gnome home.

How is an electrician like a tailor?
They both fix shorts.

What are the noisiest kind of pants?
Bell bottoms.

What can hold a car, but can't lift a feather?
  A garage.

Why did the man bring a bag of feathers to the store?
  He wanted to make a down payment.

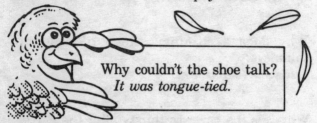

Why couldn't the shoe talk?
It was tongue-tied.

Why wouldn't the ocean talk to the lake?
  Because he thought the lake was too shallow.

Why don't berries like to be picked?
  They wind up in a jam.

Why did the girl carry her bike for ten miles?
  Because they were both tireless.

Why didn't the man like being in the kitchen?
  He found the cheese grating and he hated to hear the kettle spouting off.

What's the most important thing to hold when you dive into the Amazon River?
  Your breath.

What goes up and down but always stays in the same place?
  A seesaw.

Why did the little girl put night clothes on her cat?
She thought they were the cat's pajamas.

Why wouldn't the little girl get on the merry-go-round?
She didn't want to be taken for a ride.

What's the handiest kind of tree?
The palm.

What's everyone's favorite tree?
The poplar (popular).

What kind of tree never gets planted?
A shoe tree.

What kind of pipe never contains tobacco?
A pitch pipe.

Why did the boy decide to let his hair grow?
He couldn't figure out a way to stop it.

What's the hardest thing to hold when you're angry?
Your temper.

Why was the bird-lover carrying a bag of worms?
Just for a lark.

Why did the lady keep putting her hand up to her ear?
She wanted to hear her diamond ring.

Why did the boy pour paint on himself?
His mother told him to put on a coat.

In what kind of pool is it impossible to swim?
A car pool.

Why did the silly kid put an alarm clock in his shoe?
Because he didn't want his foot to fall asleep.

Why did the boy wear his cowboy outfit to school?
The teacher told the class they were going to learn to draw.

Why was the boy afraid of the computer?
He thought it might byte.

Why did the woman spray insect repellent on her computer?
The program had a bug in it.

How are school hallways like computers?
They both have monitors.

How are computers like coffee shops?
They both have menus.

Why didn't the woman want to put snow tires on her car?
She was afraid they'd melt.

Where do fireflies keep their cars?
In sparking lots.

When do needles get along with each other?
When they see eye to eye.

Why don't jockeys work very hard?
They're too busy horsing around.

Why did the airline passenger demand a parachute?
He heard he was on a non-stop flight.

What fruit is never by itself?
Pears.

Why did the lady iron her clothes so often?
She wanted to be known as one of the ten best pressed women.

Why was the teller fired from the bank?
He didn't have enough cents.

Why was the vampire asked to join Little League?
He had all the bats.

Why did the captain bring his ship to the hospital?
Because someone told him to take it to the dock.

Where can you find counterintelligence?
At the deli.

How important are Einstein's theories?
Relatively.

Non-Fiction Bestseller List

1. *The Forty-Niners*
   by Seymour Gold

2. *The Jungle and Me*
   by Chip Anzee

3. *Is Adoption for You?*
   by B. R. Childe

4. *Your Garden and You*
   by G. Ranium

5. *America's Longest River*
   by Mrs. Hippy

6. *Behind Bars* by Gil T.

7. *Take Care of #1*
   by Sal Fish

8. *Personal Grooming*
   by Harry Leggs

9. *Christmas Customs*
   by Miss L. Toe

10. *Magic Tricks*
    by Annie Card

Old _____ Never Die,
They Just _____

Old accountants never die, they just lose their figures.

Old teachers never die, they just lose their class.

Old librarians never die, they just go out of circulation.

Old doctors never die, they just lose their patients.

Old directors never die, they just fade out.

Old principals never die, they just lose their faculties.

Old poets never die, they just get verse and verse.

Old garbage men never die, they just go to waste.

Old ball players never die, they just strike out.

Old gymnasts never die, they just tumble around.

Old card sharks never die, they just lose the deal.

Old shoppers never die, they just go buy buy.

Old Italians never die, they just Rome around.

Old owls never die, they just don't give a hoot.

Old chimney cleaners never die, they just go up in smoke.

Old train engineers never die, they just get sidetracked.

Old fishermen never die, they just lose their mussels.

Old dancers never die, they just shuffle off to Buffalo.

Old firemen never die, they just burn out.

Old farmers never die, they just go to seed.

Old roofers never die, they just hang up their shingles.

Old drivers never die, they just run out of gas.

Old boaters never die, they just drift away.

Old stamp collectors never die, they just get cancelled.

Old bankers never die, they just lose their cents.

Old carpenters never die, they just get board.

Old electricians never die, they just blow a fuse.

Old magazine editors never die, they just lose their circulation.

Old arm wrestlers never die, they just lose their grip.

Old clock makers never die, they just run out of time.

Old railroad conductors never die, they just get off track.

Old upholsterers never die, they just run for cover.

Old winemakers never die, they just go sour.

Old gunslingers never die, they just bite the bullet.

Old milkmaids never die, they just kick the bucket.

Old cooks never die, they just run out of thyme.

Old housepainters never die, they just get plastered.

Old animal trainers never die, they just go to the dogs.

Old dairy farmers never die, they just lose their whey.

Old matches never die, they just lose their heads.

Old canners never die, they just flip their lids.

Old bakers never die, they just toss their cookies.

Old tennis players never die, they just get into a different racket.

Old streetcar drivers never die, they just go off the rails.

Old tanners never die, they just go into hiding.

Old tightrope walkers never die, they just lose their balance.

Old kings never die, they just get throne away.

Old mimes never die, they're just never heard from again.

Old baseball players never die, they just get thrown out.

Old drivers never die, they just turn into garages.

Old astronauts never die, they just space out.

Paperback Bestseller List

1. *Mexican Cooking*
   by N. Chilada

2. *Woman's Guide to Romance*
   by Mary A. Mann

3. *Things You Shouldn't Eat* by Al Ergic

4. *My Secret* by Diz Closed

5. *I Hate People* by Leif Mia Lone

6. *How to Dress for the Jungle*
   by Dan D. Lyon

7. *I Can Do Anything*
   by Barry Abel

8. *Smart People*
   by I.M.A. Genius

9. *Give Me Your Money*
   by Emma Swindler

10. *Ouch!*
    by Charlie Horse

8
Famous Last Words

"Come on, *Jaws* was just a movie."

"Let's go swimming. Who's afraid of a little lightning?"

"Lightning never strikes twice in the same spot."

"I'm just going to light the pilot."

"The gun isn't loaded."

"I just had the brakes fixed."

"It's okay, Franco never misses when he throws the knives."

"Sure I'll put the apple on my head, Dad."

"I'll put my ear to the rail to hear if the train's coming."

"Shucks, General Custer, there isn't an Indian within a hundred miles."

"I raised this lion from a kitten . . . She wouldn't hurt a soul."

"See, I'm not afraid of heights."

"I'm pretty sure this is water."

"Bears are more afraid of us than we are of them."

"Don't be such a scaredy cat, this isn't a poisonous snake."

"I'm sure we can settle this peacefully."

"So the can has a dent in it . . . I'm hungry."

"Of course I turned off the gas."

"I can kill that lion bare-handed."

"Don't worry, the power's off."

ACROBAT: "Like my new handcream?"

DRIVER: "I can take this turn with my eyes closed."

LION TAMER: "I think I fed them this morning."

CAMPER: "Taste this new kind of mushroom I found."

BUILDER: "This time let's put up the roof first."

CAMPER: "If you've seen one snake you've seen 'em all."

ABE LINCOLN: "Hurry, we don't want to be late for the theater."

NURSE: "I don't think it's contagious."

Shaggy Sheep Story

Early one morning a sheep herder was moving his flock from one pasture to another when something frightened the animals. They bolted onto the road, and nothing the shepherd did could bring them under control. He was worried because soon the morning traffic would be upon them. As he became more and more frantic, a truck rounded the bend. It stopped suddenly in front of the running sheep and a suitcase fell out of the back. The shepherd stared in amazement as his flock stopped running and walked slowly across the road. As the driver of the truck got out to retrieve his suitcase, the shepherd said that was the most amazing thing he'd ever seen. The driver replied, "I've always been told I had a case that could stop a flock."

9
Tom Swifties

"I can play the flute," Tom piped up.

"That hinge needs oiling," Tom squeaked.

"Use this sandpaper," Tom said roughly.

"I wake up before the roosters," Tom crowed.

"I have to go to a funeral tomorrow," Tom said gravely.

"No charge," Tom gave off freely.

"I'm bored," Tom said flatly.

"Give me the reins," Tom said hoarsely.

"There's a snake in that hole," Tom hissed.

"My blue jeans have fallen off," Tom panted.

"Where's my jacket?" Tom asked coolly.

"Don't throw that pan at me," Tom flew off the handle.

"Stop right now," Tom stated haltingly.

"What is one minus one?" Tom quizzed naughtily.

"I love hockey," Tom said puckishly.

"I'm frozen," Tom said stiffly.

"You broke my pencil," Tom said pointlessly.

"What a beautiful brook," Tom babbled.

"You've taken my dough," Tom's voice rose kneadlessly.

"Give me my knife," Tom said sharply.

"I love lemons," Tom said tartly.

"You'll ruin the picture," Tom snapped negatively.

"I have to go to the doctor," Tom said patiently.

"I have a temperature," Tom said feverishly.

"That must be a terrier," Tom said doggedly.

"See you at midnight," Tom replied darkly.

"She lives so far away," Tom said distantly.

"Can't this horse go faster?" Tom said ploddingly.

"There's a storm coming," Tom thundered.

"I'm counting on you," Tom added.

"Hyenas live in Africa," Tom laughed.

"I can play the piano," Tom said grandly.

"I always thought I should be king," Tom said regally.

"You're such a complainer," Tom moaned.

"You're in the army now," Tom said militantly.

"I need new clothes," Tom said raggedly.

"That's how the cookie crumbles," Tom chipped in.

"Have some candy," Tom snickered.

"That's not allowed," Tom said forbiddingly.

"I hate storms," Tom raged.

"I like crunchy apples," Tom stated crisply.

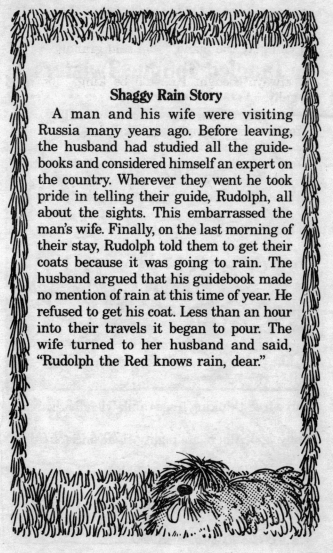

Shaggy Rain Story

A man and his wife were visiting Russia many years ago. Before leaving, the husband had studied all the guide-books and considered himself an expert on the country. Wherever they went he took pride in telling their guide, Rudolph, all about the sights. This embarrassed the man's wife. Finally, on the last morning of their stay, Rudolph told them to get their coats because it was going to rain. The husband argued that his guidebook made no mention of rain at this time of year. He refused to get his coat. Less than an hour into their travels it began to pour. The wife turned to her husband and said, "Rudolph the Red knows rain, dear."

10
Tangled Tongue Twisters

Say them three times quickly.

Three free-thinking frogs think friendly thoughts.

Anny and Albert ate eighty-eight ancient eggs.

Big bad Bobby bragged and blustered.

Shimmering ships sailed the seas.

Big boys boot baby buggies.

Rotten Roscoe rescued Rosie from the roaring rapids.

Ugly Ursula ushered urchins.

Into, out of, over, under, Egberth tried to hide from thunder.

Jimmy Jack Hackett jilted Jill Brackett.

Six shy sisters sort short socks.

Bright Brenda Bop popped Bob's big balloon.

He bought fish sauce at the fish sauce shop.

Three free thoughtful seals.

Free-falling flight.

Greg grows gallons of green gleaming grapes.

The class brash lass crashed.

See Shep slip.

Trim these three fine free trees.

Pretty bright pink plums.

Felix finds fresh French fries finer.

Two tiny tigers think tough thoughts.

Four fast fishermen find five fat flounders.

Simple sharks shared some shrimp.

Four fast-flying French fireflies.

Barney brought big baby booties to Barstow.

Plucky Polly performed perfectly.

Shameful sheep-sellers sell cheap sheep.

Thirsty Tina tried tricky Tim's tea.

Fred fed fifty thrifty freaks franks.

Nine new nurses nursed ninety naughty ninnies.

Bluebirds bite black bugs.

Hugh hewed yew.

Think frank thoughts freely.

Eunice's son's songs sound sour.

Rub rugs roughly.

Landlubbers love blubber.

Chester chills chicks.

Speak, sphynx.

Frieda's finicky fingers flung flies.

Shaggy Piano Tuner Story

During a world tour a concert pianist arrived in a small Swiss town early one Sunday morning. His concert was to be that afternoon, so he went immediately to inspect the piano and the stage. The stage was huge and the piano badly out of tune. The pianist could find only one piano tuner who would come out on a Sunday, Mr. Oppernockity. By early afternoon Mr. Oppernockity had tuned it perfectly. The pianist realized later that if the piano stayed where it was the audience would be unable to see him. He had the piano moved to the center of the stage. Unfortunately this caused the old piano to go out of tune again. He called Mr. Oppernockity and told him the problem. To which he received the reply, "Oppernockity tunes but once."

11
Take These Knock
Knocks—Please!

Knock knock.
Who's there?
Albie.
Albie who?
"Albie down to get you in a taxi, honey."

Knock knock.
Who's there?
Anna.
Anna who?
Anna one, anna two . . . !

Knock knock.
Who's there?
Artemus.
Artemus who?
Artemus (Artie must) come down, his ride is waiting.

Knock knock.
Who's there?
Ben.
Ben who?
Ben walkin' the dog.

Knock knock.
Who's there?
Butter.
Butter who?
Butter late than never.

KNOCK
KNOCK

Knock knock.
Who's there?
Byron.
Byron who?
Byron (buy one), get one free.

KNOCK
KNOCK

Knock knock.
Who's there?
Canary.
Canary who?
Canary come out and play?

KNOCK
KNOCK

Knock knock.
 Who's there?
Chester.
 Chester who?
Chester average guy.

Knock knock.
 Who's there?
Crab.
 Crab who?
Crab onto the door knob and open the door.

Knock knock.
 Who's there?
Dandelion.
 Dandelion who?
Dandelion you've got waiting outside your door.

Knock knock.
 Who's there?
Danette.
 Danette who?
Danette is full of da fish.

Knock knock.
 Who's there?
Darryl.
 Darryl who?
Darryl be a new day a'comin'.

Knock knock.
Who's there?
Datsun.
Datsun who?
Datsun is too hot.

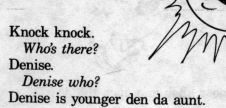

Knock knock.
Who's there?
Denise.
Denise who?
Denise is younger den da aunt.

Knock knock.
Who's there?
Eiffel.
Eiffel who?
Eiffel down the steps.

Knock knock.
Who's there?
Ermagarde.
Ermagarde who?
Ermagarde at Buckingham Palace.

Knock knock.
Who's there?
Father.
Father who?
Father down the hall is a giant tarantula.

Knock knock.
  Who's there?
Harry.
  Harry who?
Harry up and open the door.

Knock knock.
  Who's there?
Heiress.
  Heiress who?
Heiress the butter I borrowed.

Knock knock.
  Who's there?
Hugh.
  Hugh who?
Hugh tired of knock knock jokes yet?

Knock knock.
  Who's there?
Irma.
  Irma who?
Irma gettin' tired.

Knock knock.
  Who's there?
Isabel.
  Isabel who?
Isabel broken?

Knock knock.
Who's there?
Issy.
Issy who?
Issy gone yet?

Knock knock.
Who's there?
Ken.
Ken who?
Ken I come in?

Knock knock.
Who's there?
Len.
Len who?
Len me in, I'm hungry.

Knock knock.
Who's there?
Lettuce.
Lettuce who?
Lettuce in, it's cold
out here.

Knock knock.
Who's there?
Lil.
Lil who?
Lil did you know
I'd be here.

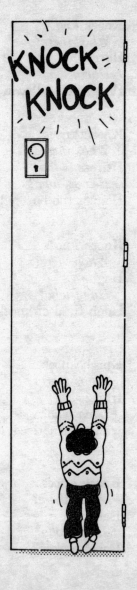

Knock knock.
Who's there?
Liz.
Liz who?
Liz'n and I'll tell you.

Knock knock.
Who's there?
Millicent.
Millicent who?
Millicent me up here to knock on your door.

Knock knock.
Who's there?
Morris.
Morris who?
Morris not enough.

Knock knock.
Who's there?
Max.
Max who?
Max no difference
who I am.

Knock knock.
Who's there?
Moll.
Moll who?
Moll shook up.

Knock knock.
Who's there?
Oliver.
Oliver who?
Oliver keys are missing.

Knock knock.
Who's there?
Parker.
Parker who?
Parker over there.

Knock knock.
Who's there?
Pecan.
Pecan who?
Pecan somebody your own size.

Knock knock.
Who's there?
Philippine.
Philippine who?
Philippine in your back? I have a new voodoo doll.

Knock knock.
Who's there?
Ron.
Ron who?
Ron get your mother.

Knock knock.
Who's there?
Rosetta.
Rosetta who?
Rosetta green apple
and got a belly ache.

Knock knock.
Who's there?
Sherwood.
Sherwood who?
Sherwood like to come in.

Knock knock.
Who's there?
Soda lady.
Soda lady who?
Quit yodelling and let me in!

Knock knock.
Who's there?
Sofa.
Sofa who?
Sofa so good.

KNOCK

Knock knock.
Who's there?
Sweater.
Sweater who?
Sweater out here
than it is inside.

Knock knock.
  Who's there?
Talia.
  Talia who?
Talia story if you let me in.

Knock knock.
  Who's there?
Theo.
  Theo who?
"Theo grey mare, she ain't what she used to be."

Knock knock.
  Who's there?
Thurber.
  Thurber who?
Thurber in the hand is worth two in the bush.

Knock knock.
  Who's there?
Watson.
  Watson who?
Watson TV tonight?

Knock knock.
  Who's there?
Who.
  Who who?
What are you, an owl?

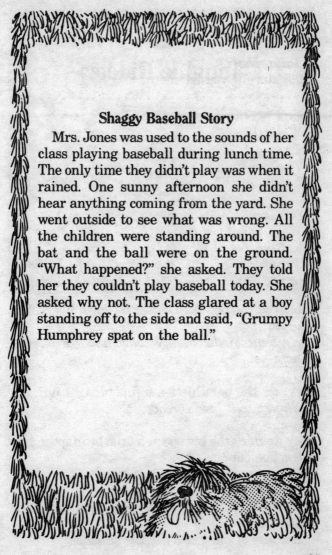

Shaggy Baseball Story

Mrs. Jones was used to the sounds of her class playing baseball during lunch time. The only time they didn't play was when it rained. One sunny afternoon she didn't hear anything coming from the yard. She went outside to see what was wrong. All the children were standing around. The bat and the ball were on the ground. "What happened?" she asked. They told her they couldn't play baseball today. She asked why not. The class glared at a boy standing off to the side and said, "Grumpy Humphrey spat on the ball."

12
Toughie Riddles

What did the pet store owner do when his rabbits escaped?

He went to the beauty salon and borrowed a hare-net.

How are the healthiest muffins brought up?

They're well bred (bread).

Why wouldn't the big spoon let the little spoon into the coffee cup?

It was just a young-stir.

Why couldn't Alice in Wonderland get out of the rabbit hole?

Because of the gravity of the situation.

Why did the baker's son become a baker like his father?

It was bread (bred) into him and he wanted to rise to the occasion.

Why did the girl get stung when she put on her coat?

It was a yellowjacket.

Why is Joe such a pain in the kitchen?

He whips the cream, strains the soup and makes the beef stew.

What do you call the dull horse that lives next door?

Your neigh-bore.

Why was the lumberjack good at math?
He knew his log rhythms (logarithms).

Why do kittens read so well?
They're litter-ary.

Why wasn't the chicken convicted of the crime?
Egg-stenuating circumstances.

Why did the orchestra stop playing?
The conductor threw his Bach out.

What did the catsup say to the bun?
The wurst (worst) is yet to come.

In what hotel room is it all right to barbecue a chicken?
"The Firebird Suite."

What did the computer programmer say to the man with the dog?

"Move your cur, sir (cursor)."

What do you call a midget wrestler?

Half Nelson.

Why do people in Nashville tie strings around their fingers?

They have a Tennessee (tendency) to forget.

Why didn't the teacher object when her classroom was so full?

She had no room to complain.

Why did the man give his wife an evergreen for her birthday?

She always wanted a fur (fir).

Why doesn't a male lion live alone?

His pride won't let him.

Shaggy Cook Story

Arnold Farnsworth, owner of the best restaurant in town, had a problem. Business was at an all-time high but two of his cooks quit to join the circus. The restaurant manager wanted to place an ad in the local paper. Arnold, however, was looking for a quicker solution. Charles, who was by far the best chef he'd ever seen, had a brother who was looking for work. Arnold insisted on hiring the brother at once, even though his manager thought it was a terrible idea. That night Charles' brother set off a grease fire, and burned the kitchen down. As Arnold Farnsworth surveyed the disaster the next morning, his manager said to him, "I was trying to tell you: you can't judge a cook by his brother."

Index

About the Authors

Meridith Berk has written comedy material for such entertainers as Debbie Reynolds, Rip Taylor and Phyllis Diller. She lives in Los Angeles with her husband, daughter and three cats. She enjoys bicycle riding, water skiing and playing the banjo.

Toni Vavrus lives and works in Los Angeles. She has written articles for horse magazines and curriculum for private schools. In addition to writing, she enjoys hanggliding, music and water sports.

About the Illustrator

Jeff Sinclair has been drawing cartoons for most of his 33 years, and has illustrated many books. He has been the winner of several local and national awards for cartooning and humorous illustration. When he's not drawing, Jeff can be found attempting to complete his basement or in his garage, working on a 1970 Mercedes 250 coupe, once driven by Warren Beatty. He lives in Vancouver, British Columbia, Canada, with his wife Karen, son Brennan and Great Dane, Probable Coz.